Praise for
OBALÚAYÉ

The poems of Jide Badmus have thrusts, intricacy, pathos. They have movement, juice, immediacy. No wonder the poems can snarl and also be tender. This poet is not afraid to imagine the ideal and confront injustice. The full force of intimate spaces—bodily and environmental—is not discounted. These sensuous and insightful poems take hold of you, involve you. In *Obalúayé*, Badmus has written poems that are like doors we can enter into. You need this book.

—**Uche Nduka**, author of *SCISSORWORK*

Jide Badmus stunning collection of raw and visceral poetry speaks volumes on the human condition. This is the kind of book that will be talked about for generations to come.

—**Natalie Sierra**, author of *Charlie, Forever and Ever*

A positive charge that grants access to the reader runs through *Obalúayé*. Jide Badmus brings fresh but keenly observed lines to the contemporary poetry coming out of Nigeria. Whether he is in the meditative vein or skirting erotic ecstasy, the controlled lyricism of this poet plunges us into the very pools of primal poetry.

—**Tade Ipadeola**, author of *The Sahara Testaments*

OBALÚAYÉ

FLOWERSONG
PRESS

by
Jide Badmus

FLOWERSONG
P R E S S

FlowerSong Press
Copyright © 2022 by Jide Badmus
ISBN: 978-1-953447-48-7
Library of Congress Control Number: 2022938982

Published by FlowerSong Press
in the United States of America.
www.flowersongpress.com

Cover Art by Martins Deep
Cover Design by Priscilla Celina Suarez
Set in Adobe Garamond Pro

NOTICE: SCHOOLS AND BUSINESSES
FlowerSong Press offers copies of this book at quantity discount with bulk
purchase for educational, business, or sales promotional use. For information,
please email the Publisher at info@flowersongpress.com.

Acknowledgements

Cliché, The Moon's Appetite, Home, Fear, reaching for light, Teaser, Extorting god, Dark Room, glass, Driver, Jesus is an Exclamation, Allergies, Skinsong, Quiet, and *Obaluaye* have appeared in in the following literary journals, magazine and anthologies: Neuro Logical, Praxis, The African Writers review, Writers Space Africa, Jalada Africa, Crepe & Penn, The Shore, The Quills, and Sub-Saharan Magazine.

For the things that plague us

CONTENTS

WIND WITHOUT MOUTH

Cliché......3

Running 4

The Moon's Appetite......5

Broken Throttle......6

Brim......7

Axe Questions......8

On Sleep......9

The Witness......10

Life Sentence......11

Home......12

A POEM HAUNTS ME

Release......15

This Poem has no Name......16

A Poem Haunts Me......17

Splintered Verses......18

Fear......19

Night......20

Nightmares......21

Ghost of Light......22

SILENCE COOKBOOK

Things I will not tell you......25

Red Eyes......26

reaching for light......28

Silence Cookbook......30

Teaser......31

The Wages of Loyalty Applying Newton's Third Law
of Motion......32

Extorting god......34

A King Away......35

Manure......36

Salt......37

A Clone of the One You Hate......38

Darkroom......39

glass......40

THEATRE OF ABSURD

driver......43

Jesus is an Exclamation......44

Absence......45

Allergies......46

The Theatre of Absurd......47

The Royal Mite......48

Mirage......49

Dust......51

Skinsong......52

Blood Song......53

No Tears......54

OBALÚAYÉ

Contagion......57

paranoia......59

androids......60

Quiet......61

Crushed......62

Breathe......63

Obalúayé......64

Introduction

Obaluaye is a poetry collection for the things that plague us. *Obaluaye* is a Yoruba god of infirmities and healing.

The poems in this book talk of cradles and graves and every experience in-between, employing the duality attribute of the Orisha of epidemics. Each poem is an experience of health and death wrapped in a pod, of strength and flaws and a thirst for things that elude.

This collection explores the human cycle—the routine of life and death (and a possibility of restoration, rebirth). It seeks to understand the things that haunt us—our fears, our nightmares, quest for freedom, the weight of responsibilities, the paradox of hope, devotion and betrayals, failed states and the covid-19 pandemic.

Obaluaye is a realization that "life is a cocktail of sweet, sour and insipid" and we are born to run this cycle, reaching for light, reaching for freedom…that ultimately leads to the grave.

WIND WITHOUT MOUTH

Cliché

Each time I walk by,
I hear the stream sing
the same song as it
washes the earth beneath &
splashes against rocks
& pebbles in its path.

Each time we make love,
our bodies become water
seeking a miracle—of gourds
& calabashes—flowing into
mouths of the gods of lust.

Each time we go to war,
we make love to destruction &
bring beauty to its knees. We
wreck innocence & shatter trust.
We embrace a lifetime of nightmares.

Each time a child is born,
he mourns the beginning of his end
while our teeth dance around bonfires.
Life is a cocktail—sweet, sour & insipid.
Living is cliché—dying, the same!

Running

The world runs in cycles—
man is locked in a loop
of time &routines
like gears running into each other
in the mind of the clock.

The human race—
is it our nature to run
like lost rats in a maze
chasing after cheese?
Hope hangs in a hoop,
dreams are unending, turning
like wheels on regurgitated paths.

The sun's fire runs into the sea,
drinks to stupor &perspires in torrents
back into the pool from which it drank.
Smiles have a way of running
into clouds of tears on life's treadmill.

The world runs in cycles
a seed dies and is reborn—
a new soul in a new body!
A chorus keeps running
as long as the song is on...

The Moon's Appetite

say, death is a parasite…
              [mirror, Pamilerin Jacob]

he chewed on our pillows,
deprived us of dreams.
he perched on your petals
& drained your smile of colour.
Now, you are trapped in reels
of monochrome memories—
lost in a city
of monologues
& sighs,
where salty smiles die in their cradles

the moon is hungry
& daughter wants to feed her
a bowl of cereal
but the moon only eats shadows
& probably had a lean appetite
the night darkness swallowed you

Broken Throttle

I.
sun in a coffin, you
needed a miracle to rise

but unbelief held the tongues
of those close to you.

you were
wind without mouth—

blind torch,
broken throttle...

II.
I drew you close—
careful not to trigger

that which could tip you over.
I kept a distance. I sought a balance.

somehow you still let the beast
sink vile teeth into you

you left unused reams of smile
at the corner of your room

& a final note of thanks
on the screen of my phone.

Brim

They say water is life,
so I fill this glass to
replenish the stream
pouring from my pores.

I peel these synthetic skins
& stand like a field without grass
under sprinkling aqueous seedlings.
I feel rigour seep through into drains beneath

I sip from her fountain of lips
& float into her depth.
I hear water splatter
on the walls within
her thighs—my grave,
my cradle.

They say water is life.
My eyes are as baskets spilling
harvest of tears—tissues
wrecked in pitiful puddles.
My soul is parched & my body aches.
So I fill this bathtub to the brim—
I need a full dose of life.

Axe Questions

We are as trees
on the field of life
pregnant with questions,
like, when is the trunk mature
enough to serve the axe-head?

On Sleep
(A response to John Keats' ON DEATH)

If death be sleep
why then do we weep?
Why don't we care to wait
for them that sleep to wake?

If life is but a dream, pain
is illusory...sweet is plain
and insipid, the same!

The Witness

his tongue is
tied to a stone,
who has seen the
face of death—
he kisses the
dust of the ground
& swears secrecy

Life Sentence

There is no hell
hot as being locked up,
trapped in space—
no vaccine effective
as the breath of freedom.

There's no freedom
for the living man—
captive in his own kingdom,
spirit caged within body
—until the body dies!

Home

home is where
peace is a perpetual baby

but every birth comes
with an umbilical to its grave

A POEM HAUNTS ME

Release

The shadows that lulled me to sleep
still fogged my eyes when I woke.

Wrinkles of worry caressed my face.
My thoughts slumped & landed

With the heavy thud of a sigh.
Hoofs of hunger tortured mental terrains.

Darkness crawled over
barren thoughts.

I begged to hear
voice of inspiration—

It came in cold currents, stiffening the
senses. Then it prickled me with pleasure.

Ideas sprouted, thoughts thickened,
mind's muscles throbbed with excitement.

My mouth tasted Vanilla smiles.
A paroxysm of poetry gripped me,

Restored the voice of my pen.
Words rushed onto white lawns

This Poem has no Name

Sometimes I christen
embryos of thoughts,
only for lips to spew
stillbirth songs
Other times,
a poem comes premature,
in need of baptism of light.

This poem came out of my mouth
with legs—didn't wait to be named

A Poem Haunts Me

I.
this dawn was born dead.

this love will not make it
out of the delivery room

my bank of words was razed
by xenophobic armies &

you come wearing masks of reprisal
to loot my emotional reserve—

you stretch this silence further

II.
you reap sleep
from unripe eyes with

sickles of thoughts—
you tickle muse.

you lurk
at the periphery of my mind—

silhouette of imagination,
you tease me with bubble kisses.

Splintered Verses

I.
I break into slivers of smiles
because this poem is heavy
& would drag me down into
exhaustive reveries—
because a smile is a poem!
I am metaphor for silhouettes—
light, cracking the spine of night
with cooing dawns & red-eyed moons.

II.
I break into shards of sighs
because these lines are drowned
in pain & I'm running out of breath—
because a sigh is ellipsis &
I'm a tide in time's test-tube,
transient—a tale yet to end...

Fear

the eloquent grope in
the dark of incoherence
like fidgeting statues.

the wind shivers,
pavements break
into sweat &
heartbeats crawl
like furious waterfalls

Night

Darkness devours light.
The bat regains sight &
the owl is back in flight.

The serene lyrics you recite,
like a lullaby, complete day's rites—
sleep takes over until the sun re-ignites.

Nightmares

On this strange bed,
willing sleep to seize
weary eyes, I turn like
restless wheels beneath
a blanket of nightmares.
I defy slumber.
Time hums
away on a static wheel.
Shadows over-take me—
I feel left behind.
It is morning &
I need to catch
up on my dreams.

Ghost of Light

Fear takes form
 of night.

The storm sometimes *cums*
in spurts of silent nightmares
& peace tumbles on
wild waves of snores.

For some, sleep is
 a lost song.

SILENCE COOKBOOK

Things I will not tell you

I hold silence
in my mouth.
Things I want
to say to you
weigh heavy
on my heart.

You sometimes see
through the picket,
the wandering wind
in my mind's backyard—
you reach for thoughts
dangling on clotheslines.
You try to unfold my body,
search for signs of worry
but I hide my fears in the
spaces between my toes.

I keep extra batteries
to power my smiles—
send the stars out to
dilute the night & find
a way to gag the sighs.
Sometimes, the burden
is mine to bear—alone.

Red Eyes

I eat caked words—
that's how I speak
to my anxiety.
I sleep like the sea.
Somehow, the storm
is asleep too.

Dawn wakes
with stale breath—
morning's mouth,
a pond of fears
from yesterday
& the days before.

By the window,
I hold a mug & sip
on the orange sun.
The cock standing
on one leg, is he
nervous or cautious?
Do you also lace your
prayer with caffeine
& hope it doesn't lose
steam midway?

I need a dose of
something stronger
than hope..but the
red of the eyes
only camouflages
stalking silhouettes.
Mountains are not
moved by courage
nor tears.

It's another day,
yet, yesterday's
misery hugs me
like ticks behind
a dog's ears.
I can't free myself!

reaching for light

my first time at the
Sunway Pyramids,

i walked down
an ascending escalator

in my head. i know
one man who would go

through with such impulse
—a tipsy Max once sang

a love song to
a stranger in the elevator.

when i'm bored, i sit
in the mall & watch

people ride the escalator—smile
at memories of little brother

sneaking up on automatic doors
at the Sheraton. in this darkness,

we constantly reach out for
a ray—spark of laughter,

blue skies in pockets
of clouds.

they say there is light
at the end of the tunnel—

but we have on our hands
a growing tunnel or a

light receding like my hairline.
hope is a woman,

bald—this wig on her
head will not grow a strand.

Silence Cookbook

Kiss my voice like rock wool—
sip my words into your hollow
& spit them back as echoes.

Teaser

you opened the earth above
my seed of hope

& virgin stem leapt into the
embrace of promissory rays

but how did you manage to
wrap up bubbles as a gift?

expectation ate me
as the sun, shadows

& your voice grew
mold & frost—

it's winter here where we
last had a warm conversation.

The Wages of Loyalty Applying Newton's Third Law of Motion

I.
What is the complexion of loyalty?

I feel blue, washed,
hanging under your weather.
Why do I long for songs
from a tongue that constantly punches
holes in my laughter?
Why do I give my all to a future
that, as bubble gum only dances
between your selfish teeth—
promises that taste like fermented piss.
Your sun shines on everyone but me.

I feel brown,
parched, praying for rain.
Why do you hold over me an umbrella?
Why does your smile smell
patronising
& deceptive
& disdainful?
Why do I remain in perpetual naivety,
gazing at *my star* in your distant sky?

II.
How do you come to terms with a god
who blesses your sacrifice with denial
& treats your offering with distrust?
How do you show that your sun is
awake behind night's scene—that
your commitment is a rooster

or a wall clock?

How do you realign
unrequited allegiance?

Extorting god

I.
How quickly the warmth of your worship cooled into a mist. How easily
our altar accumulated dust. Your mask of loyalty slipped like the sun into
the horizon at the death of day. I remember how you pelted the earth
with libations & spilled my name in a mantra—poured oil on my feet &
filled the air with fragrant smiles. How you called me father, wore me like
a pendant—tucked me in your heart like the scripture.

II.
*This idol is a glutton—set before him a buffet of adulation & waltz into his
heart. If that fails, offer tears as ablution to invoke mercy.*

You try to fit god between your palms but he's as a bubble. You sink your
teeth into waters of supplication, falling as desperate tides against my hull
but I am *Olumo,* unmoved by your antics.

A King Away

My head is a desert.
This concert has no voice.

I'm seated here,
listening to the wind

sing—a body of dust
moves to the rhythm

& brings tears to the eyes
of dance.

I find my way through
crowded emotions

gathered outside my window.
You see me lounging

in green fields
from the comfort of

your shiny console—
I have built

a mansion from this
pile of debris, *abi*?

Imagine the solar king,
prisoner of night.

I am here, seated on a Sahara
of unfathomable treasures—

a king away from home.

Manure

You put my head down
between your thighs,
palms funnel into
my mouth. I struggle.
Hope tastes like wood
shavings—still, I won't let
you force-feed me despair.

Growth comes from
a place of decadence.
I turn the hate you dump
at my backyard into manure.
The rock tears in silence,
a flower doesn't wear frowns
—yea, I will crack my lips like
peanut pods &
let a smile pop.

Salt

I am salt inside water—
broken, lost, wandering
The plains of your face.
I tell a tale of your pain.
This memory breathes,
unwanted, unloved—seed
from the devil's loins,
today's proof of yesterday
& the war you succumbed to.

A Clone of the One You Hate

Can a woman forget her sucking child that she should not have compassion on the son of her womb? (Isaiah 49:15)

I am mortar,
aching at your kneading...needing.
This love you force on me is tasteless—
I hold a lump in my throat
& choke from within.
I am shackled to your rusty tongue
& the filth that rolls off its cliff.
You whine like the old ceiling fan in my room—
about everything & nothing.
Your words are knives.
I call you mother but you feed me venom!
I'm like moon eaten half by your sky.
I keep questioning my alter if I'm truly your only—
maybe I carry the face of the one you so hate,
perhaps you punish me for father's sins.

Darkroom

I'm at the riverbank,
fishing for memories

but the line comes up empty
—not one moment of a smile

not meant for the camera!
Your love is twilight, tepid

—your anger,
a vibrant waterfall.

Father told me not to read
too much to the sun's temper,

to see light rather than wrath
But you're not the sun,

you are dry wind,
warhorse for sandstorms.

Mother said you are rain,
I should embrace you

like the sea—but
you beat me

with furious tongues
—I ripple in silence.

I'm at the riverbank,
fishing—it's getting late

& not one room of your
memory left a light on.

glass

this poem reaches for
my heart, exhumes

the remains of a song.
there is no sound.

I can't find a worthy
synonym for silence.

or distance. or bitterness.
how do dead things grow?

we tend to forget a leaking roof
until the rains arrive—again.

a grudge isn't wished away,
a grudge isn't washed away.

i'm tired of your blind axe
tearing me to splinters,

of burning in the
hell of your tongue.

there is an unopened
bottle of forgiveness

on my breakfast table
but there's only one glass

& i have lost my appetite.

THEATRE OF ABSURD

driver

the road is
full of mouths
& everything is
out to eat you.

stuck in the
jaws of traffic,
thirsty—a cold
bottle of water
sells for double
its normal price
on the long bridge.

engine overheats.
you still need the
overpriced water
for the radiator.

& when you think
you have broken
free of traffic,
police palms open
—like tithe bags—
on potholed altars.

the road is
full of mouths
& everything is
out to eat you.

Jesus is an Exclamation

where I live, emergency
service is on life support—
the fireman's truck tank is empty
& the ICU needs blood & electricity.
perhaps that's why we have learnt to
call on Jesus when in distress
or in shock or bemused,
because ours is a land of absurdities
& our mouths are yet to find
a more fitting exclamation.

Absence

I.
Daylight is a poem
in the mouth of the sun.

Dawn is visual innuendo—
light in bed with night.

Silhouettes testify to an
ever present, never sleeping,

never dying lamp in the sky.

II.
Not all things not seen
are absent—not all

things buried are dead.
The tree stands, without feet,

heart in the earth.
In my country, we hide

stolen money in dry wells
& join the masses to sing

a hymn of dry mouths.

Allergies

I.
I warn my mouth
not to squander smiles
because tears are stored as
ice cubes in lachrymal trays
& rain is bound to crash
an open air party

II.
Here, electricity is
allergic to wind & water!

III.
The lame does not die
in a forecasted war...
but where I come from we
don't smell the leaking gas
—super firemen, we pray
for a miracle of rain
to thwart the fire.

The Theatre of Absurd

The black blood in her veins is the genesis of her woes.
Peace—if it was ever here—left with the colonial train.

Masked perpetually, she learned to live with a pandemic
—a beautifully conceived error, an abusive relationship.
Greedy winds immobilize her, gags her sons with folktales
of snakes & monkeys richer than kings, emissary fires &
errant storms—of justice in a rocking chair, senile as a fog.

Priests have smeared their collars with the king's soup,
lies trickle down their beards as prophesies—the oracle
is corrupt! The activist positions himself for auction—
swallows a rock when the paycheque is at stake.

The sun cannot hold a grudge.
The same way, we seem to forget
our reflection in time's mirror—
same way histories get muddled,
same way we flap fantasy wings
after drowning memories in drunk smiles.

We work the farm & scavenge the bins.
& kiss the ring fingers of the oppressors
—after all, the vulture only eats the dead!

The Royal Mite

You swallow the sun
& make us feed on
crumbs of light
falling from
your mouth.
You serve a
slice of smile
in a plate of agony
& drop coins of hope
in filthy bowls of alms.

Mirage

I.
These bottlenecks where you
erstwhile navigated with ease—
this plastic scarcity—were cooked
in your kitchen.
You are the chef of our miseries!
This hope we sang about as kids
have refused to come—tomorrow
is a mirage. We remain youth
in perpetuity, leaders
in our dreams.

II.
Shit is being wrapped—again.
Another image, shoved
in our minds' oven.
The blogs flood our space
with his profile—perfect
like that of the fraud
in the federal palace.
Old magicians, same old tricks.
How do we not see
through walls of sentiments
erected over the years
—of regions & religions?
How do we keep falling for
glass smiles?

III.
You incarcerate dreams
but we have learned
to walk between these
walls, confined only to

the open space beyond.
(or have we?)
We sing solemn sighs
but our tongues—in secret—
learn laughter's lyrics.
We climb uphill with groaning
gears—eager wings
spreading behind.
Open palms pray
on foreign altars—
these dreams need visas to fly!

Dust

In this room, under my pillow
is a junkyard of broken dreams.

Here, a dilapidated bridge stalls
my feet from kissing the future.

Time is a serial killer—leaves invisible
footprints & uncountable body count.

They say sleep is a highway to penury
& time is a fast-walker who never tires

So, I run round the clock
clutching tattered aspirations.

In this land, dreams are
dust—dead on delivery!

Skinsong
(after Niyi Osundare)

*On September 1st, 2019, Nigerians came under xenophobic attacks in
Pretoria, Johannesburg & surrounding areas*

This chest has embraced dust
where memories used to nest

before *kleptomanic* winds
whisked them to foreign lands.

It is yet night
& this tongue of dawn hasn't tasted light.

We've become poisoned seeds—boil
on skin—no-one wants us on their soil.

But the enemy now wears our skin—
the monster we fight now is within.

Blood Song

A scream was strangled into flailing whispers.
A dream got smothered on its pillow.
Can laughter breathe in a land submerged in blood
—where silence is prelude to pounding metals & shattered bodies?
Can the earth grow souls from young bodies planted in them—
won't hatred sprout from a field that once bred warmth?
The sun might never be able to rescue rainbows buried in toxic clouds.
Eyes may never know the taste of sound sleep again!

No Tears

Words have walked
down this lane severally,
to a dead end where pain
exhausted its synonyms.
The weight these lean lines carry
      are of tears fighting gravity!

OBALÚAYÉ

Contagion

I.
I do not watch the news
—it breaks me.

A square-faced reporter,
with a curt smile, speaks of loss.

Darkness reaches through
the TV screen & shreds me

into creases & ripples—flakes
of empathy.

There's a commercial break.
But violence's teeth never go

on recess. Weather forecasts
tell me nature loses control too.

Viruses cross borders
without visas—

we learn to distrust smiles.
& handshakes. & hugs.

Eyes walk the night
in search of sanctuary—

where grief isn't
a bed of storms.

But trauma is a contagion—
images from the news at noon

grow voices & become
recurring nightmares.

II.
I do not write
my pains on my face

neither do I wear
a mask in denial.

I shed dead weights—
I will not carry a grave

on my shoulders—wash the
taste of sorrow in my mouth

with freshly brewed black coffee,
sit on the couch with my cat

—except I don't have one
& I'm in love with puppies—

& write a poem about cats,
coffee & a weather for lovers.

paranoia

now that we can't speak
the language that daily
heals us, we die
we die for touches
for fabrics warmer
than words
we fear strangers a little
more—at this bus park,
a beggar tapped me
twice, I flinched inside.
I let fly vocal knives
when she made to
touch me a third time.

androids

we can't interface
the way we used to
you are bruising but i
can't touch—
not even my own face
we are strangers
in love, servitude
to fear & doubts
there's a glitch in our
software—*walahi*!
humanity is dying—we
can't even check for pulse

Quiet

Church bells have grown beards
of dust. The markets are denuded.
Pigeons have taken over the parks.
We stopped calling the days by name.
Today is *abiku*—yesterday replayed—
tomorrow will wear this same face.
This quiet is of a wound festering,
a dream decaying. This silence is
of a love withering, craving the bliss
of tending—a touch of sunlight or rain.

Crushed

Days are void of light.
Nights wear wide grins.

Cruel clouds wash
the sun off the sky.

Horny hands yank
colour off riant petals.

You crush sanity with the
club between your thighs

Once upon a cherished pudding,
a wild struggle, a plundering...

Breathe

...darkness was over the surface of the deep... —Genesis 1: 2

We are at the mercy
   of choking knees
   & justice whose head is
   perpetually turned away.
   White lives matter...too
   Really! What gender is
   your apology?

We can't breathe.
   Our brothers ate sour grapes
   but it's our teeth that ache.
   We hide our faces, hush...we
   don't say our names in public!

We don't mention the alphabets
   between the thighs.
   Sex is sacred. But
   rebel penises have
   invaded the streets
   & we can't differentiate
   the monsters from men.

We can't breathe.
   Mama shouldn't see
   her son this helpless.
   Father, the earth is formless
   & void, all I see is darkness—
   let there be light!

Obalúayé

You held the sun
by the throat,

made love to darkness.
She screamed your name

—but your name, *Sopona*,
is not to be spoken—

we fell to the
wrath of earth.

The air we breathe
stalks us.

Water can't cleanse this curse.
You are death,

you are antidote.
The sun is your wife,

The moon, your concubine.
The world is hungry for light.

The streets
are dying for your healing sweep.

About the Author

Jide Badmus is an engineer, a poet inspired by beauty and destruction; he believes that things in ruins were once beautiful.

He is the author of *There is a Storm in my Head*; *Scripture*; *Paper Planes in the Rain*; *Paradox of Little Fires*; *Silk Psalms*; and *Anatomy of the Sun* (and everything beneath). He has a Pushcart Prize nomination

Badmus has curated and edited several anthologies such as *Vowels Under Duress*; *Coffee*; *Today, I Choose Joy*; and *How to Fall in Love*.

He is the founder of INKspiredNG, Poetry Editor for Con-scio Magazine, and sits on the board of advisors for Libretto Magazine.

Jide writes from Lagos, Nigeria. He tweets @bardmus